SOME NOTES ON CORYLUS NUTS

BY

WALFORD SCOTT GREEN

Illustrations, photographs and preface by Roger Green.
Foreword by Gillian Jones. Research by Jonathan Green.

Published by Berberis Books

ISBN 9780954376895

Walford Scott Green was born in 1908 in Bishops Stortford in the county of Essex. He was educated at The Leys School and Emanuel College, Cambridge. He joined his cousin in law practice in the City of London, first under Articles and later as Partner. It was the same firm of Hanbury, Whitting and Ingle to which he returned after service in the RNVR during World War II. In 1946 with a family of two about to become three he decided that space in the countryside of Kent was a necessary part of the survival kit for the city worker and to this end he purchased the freehold of Merrimans, Ivy Hatch in the Parish of Ightham, together with some three acres of mixed Kent cobnuts. The lawns had become victory gardens of mixed vegetables and the untended nut bushes had grown up to fifteen feet or more. Work on restoring the balance of nature with the ordered design of a country house garden was delayed by the memorable cold winter of 1947, but once started and with the aid of the knowledgeable old inhabitants of Ivy Hatch, the cobs soon became healthy and productive again, the 150 year old trees seemingly immune to a few years of neglect. For 36 years the nuts were tended with the greatest of care; old ones grubbed up and new ones planted. He was a great observer and recorder and this essay is an important record of a small part of our agricultural scene that may not be with us for much longer. He died in September 1984, an autumn that as it turned out was one of the best for the nut crop and even better for the apples of Merrimans, some of which like the Russet and Beauty of Bath had not born fruit for many a year.

Foreword

Walford Green wrote his monograph on Kentish Cobnuts in 1983. It has been treasured by the family and provided happy memories of growing up in the Kent countryside with two acres of cobnuts to roam around in and help with the picking when harvest time came round each year. More recently we began to think of reproducing his work as a small booklet on the subject.

Much of the knowledge contained in these pages came from local maps and doubtless from conversations with 'locals' in the Plough at Ivy Hatch where 'Pop' Smith presided over saloon and public bars and exchanges took place between the two areas. There would have been other owners of cobnuts – at the saloon end one supposes, and those who were handy with pruning knife and 'wanning hoe' at the public end; such was the custom in those days. There was correspondence with the Royal Horticultural Society and the East Malling Research Station; Ministry of Agriculture bulletins and leaflets are also quoted. We are not aware that he was in touch with the larger commercial growers in the county and the Kentish Cobnuts Association, which brought many growers together, did not come into existence until 1991. There are certain 'facts' which he claims which have since been disproved, such as that the variety Kent Cob is self-fertile, and that the shield bug has a 'snout' like that of a weevil. We have chosen not to change what he has written but to point out the context in which it was written: a combination of local knowledge with a lot of serious research - and by the way: how many of us have actually seen a weevil's snout to compare it with a shield bug?

I am sorry that the writer, for all his dedication to his cobnut trees, is sceptical about their flavour. I think he never tried them roasted, when their flavour is beyond compare and I recommend them. Finally, I regret to say that the Merrimans cobnut trees are no longer in existence, having been grubbed up in 2018.

At a recent meeting of the KCA one member pointed out there must be a wealth of local knowledge about Kentish cobnuts which should be saved and recorded before it slipped away. This booklet is our family's contribution to that record.

Gillian Jones, Chair, Kentish Cobnuts Association. 2022

Introduction

I have been encouraged to fill the wet winter days in 1982/3 by putting together a few notes on Corylus nuts. I can make no claim to write as an horticultural expert, or as a trained scientific observer and my access to authorities, where authorities exist, has been limited. Any entitlement to write at all rests on my own experience, extending now over 36 years, tending a mixed plantation of Cobnuts and Filberts at Merrimans, Ivy Hatch, in the Parish of Ightham in the County of Kent. During such period I have, I hope, learnt something of my subject from what I have seen for myself, what I have learnt from others and from what I have been able to glean from the written word.

Let it be said from the outset that for conflict between the opinions of experts and beliefs of individual growers it is hard to beat all aspects of the story of Corylus nuts. Where agreement exists it is the exception rather than the rule. Indeed it was initial disbelief on my part on seeing in print the statement that the Cobnut as we know it came to England from Turkey at the same time as the Horse Chestnut which put me on the inquiry as to the geographical origins and varietal development of the genus.

Historical and Economic

What nobody can deny is that Corylus the hazel nut of our hedgerows has in a very similar form a world-wide distribution in the temperate zones of the Northern Hemisphere. How far back the story goes, none can say but it is not unreasonable to suppose that, as the ice age retreated, liberating northern Europe and Asia from its grip, Corylus somehow arrived and spread.

The "late arrival" theory conflicted with my own belief that Corylus in the form of our own indigenous hazel nut had a much longer history, though the varietal development from it, for the most part, came about in more recent times. Certainly Corylus was known to our Anglo-Saxon forebears as evidenced by the very clear derivation of the name from the Anglo Saxon "haesel", the word used for a hood or helmet, and "Knuttu", a nut. In its original wild form this appears never to have exceeded the height of a low growing bush of between ten and twenty feet.

Today one associates the wild hazel mainly with the hedgerows of the fields and orchards of the countryside. That is a relatively modern use and a valuable one, as a hazel hedgerow does provide a measure of wind protection to any tender growth within its confines; but until the rapid growth of the enclosure movement in the latter part of the 18th century, and as far back as sheep were folded on the common wastes of the country, the wild hazel was a coppice plant. Sheep and the wool which came from them were basic to the economy of medieval England, since thence came much of its wealth, and the hurdles made from the split rods of the hazel were essential to the folding of the flocks.

Certainly by the end of the reign of Edward IV a hazel coppice was recognized by Statute as a valuable form of property as in the last year of his reign an early Enclosure Act was passed enabling a Manorial Lord to enclose woodland and waste for a 7-year period of growth when planted with hazel, 7 years being the growth period allowed between coppicing. [1][2]

It was still the traditional belief in certain parts of the country that if certain hazel coppices are not cut at the end of every 7 years, those retaining rights of Common, become entitled to break down hedges and fences and allow their beasts to run. [3]

I have found no evidence to show that in medieval days any great importance was attached to the actual nut itself, no doubt the wild nut was then much as we know it today, sometimes plentiful, sometimes not. No doubt, too, it was in years of plenty sought by the boys and girls of the old English village communities, just as it is by our country children today.

So much for nuts in this country based on what is known of the rural economy of medieval England, and in the context of its sheep. But what of nuts elsewhere maintaining our assumption that all over the northern parts of Europe the hazel flourished? As in England, crafts were developed and country craftsmen were to be found making use of the pliable wands and stronger poles to supply local needs. Known products, to name but a few, were fish traps, lobster pots, mole traps, splints to hold down basket tops, cask hoops and walking sticks, pea sticks and bean poles, fascines for drainage purposes and bundles for use as ships fenders, as faggots for heating the baker's oven and no doubt many others to accord with the need of any particular area for a tough pliable cane. It

1 An Enclosure Act of 1483.
2 Eleven years for sweet chestnut.
3 In Dorset in 1940, but a mistaken view now in the absence of registration under the Commons Act.

seems unlikely, however, that any scientific attempt was made to improve the size and quality of the nut itself. Hybridization is a latter-day art, though that it not to say that bigger and better nuts did not come into existence from time to time as the outcome of haphazard cross fertilization.

Theophrastus (372 - 287 BC) of the School of Aristotle, in his work *Enquiry into Plants* made a distinction for the first time between woody and herbaceous plants, with a reference to Heracleatic Nuts, "some being round and some bearing a long nut", being nuts which grew around Heraclea on the southern shores of the Black Sea. [4] [5] At an earlier date Hippocrates (460 - 357 BC) appears to refer to the same nuts as Carya Thusia.

Four hundred years later Pliny (Secundus Gaius) in the *Historica Naturalis*, makes reference to Avellana in the context of these nuts, said by him to have come from Avellana in Asia Minor. It can hardly be coincidental that the nut growing area in Italy is to be found in Campania, based on the town of Avellino just to the east of Naples.

Turning from the realm of the written word to that of art, it is interesting to find that Carlo Crivelli, a Venetian of the 15th century of the school of Antonio Murano, portrays a bunch of these nuts in a Primitive work, said by Bunyard, in 1919, to be in Berlin. This, he records, shows nuts which in size, shape and habit agree very closely with the cultivated nuts which we know today. Perhaps it is also significant to recall that marine archaeologists of the

---

4 *Bunyard, Royal Horticultural Journal 1919.*
5 *Now Ponderachi; not to be confused with the many other Heraclea of which there seem to have been as many as seven around the Mediterranean Sea in those days.*

present century have, when salving Amphorae from sunken wrecks of Tome or Phoenician galleys, found that in some of them were remains of much the same type of nut. Maybe, like everything else, they were endowed with curative powers. Even before Culpepper it was said for a cold in the head: "Take small note kernels and roost him and ete him with a lytyl powder of pepyr when thou goest to bed".

Supported by the foregoing, there is enough justification for propounding the theory that what we know as the common hedgerow hazel nut was a bush indigenous to most of the temperate zones of Northern Europe and Asia from earliest days. Larger, though in fairness no more succulent nuts were to be found growing in the fertile crescent of Asia Minor: and these migrated along the Mediterranean trade routes and became established in Central Italy, at the latest by the first century A.D. spreading thence along the northern Mediterranean shores and northward into what is now Germany. In earliest days vegetative propagation was no problem, and it was not for another 1800 years that scientific hybridization permitted the meld of the northern wilding with the southern Avellana, so as to produce the varieties of the species Corylus we know today.

The Botany

This is a subject in which I have received no scientific training, and have had to glean from the knowledge and writings of others. Consequently, I write with some trepidation that my lack on the definition of the words used at the sources may lead me into what to those more erudite may find an irritating mixture of words and foolish errors. The following may perhaps be useful:

ORDER

FAGACEAE Being that monoclinous type of tree which bears flowers of both sexes.

GENUS

CORYLUS (Greek: Korus, A hood or helmet).

SPECIES

AVELLANA Being a shrub or small tree growing to an average height of 10 feet.

CALIFORNICA Being much the same.

COLURNA or the Turkish or Constantinople Nut, being a tree growing to a height of 80ft.

Save for brief references, it is to C. Avellana that these notes attempt to deal, since the term covers the whole field from the original wildling to the round or long nuts of the Euxine which have given rise to the multiplicity of varieties we know today. We still have our round and long nuts as Theophrastus knew, though somewhere along the line the parentage of many of ours, may well have been mutated by the introduction of the wild hazel strain, giving them the ability to withstand the greater rigours of the more northern winters.

The round nut is distinguished by the fact that the nut itself is held in an open cup, retained only by the abscission layer. This is correctly known to us as a Cob.

The long nut, whose cup extends out into a husk which can totally obscure the nut itself and retain it upon the tree after the abscission layer of the shell has parted is the Filbert.

Whatever the botanists may say the Men of Kent or Kentish men when making their plantings on either side of the Medway during the 18th and 19th centuries firmly named the product of their labours the Kent or Kentish Cob and this notwithstanding the fact that the major variety planted was Lambert's Filbert, a long and well-enclosed nut, a true Filbert and not a Cob at all. For purposes of differentiation hereafter let us refer to both Cobs and Filberts planted in Kent or elsewhere as Kent Cobs.

The Nomenclature

Cobnuts and Filberts, how did these names arise? One can only speculate. If a cob, in terms equestrian, be a small round horse or pony why should not a small round nut be a cob as well? Alternatively, local legend tells us that there was once a Rector of our nut-growing parish of Ightham whose name was Cobb who tended a plantation of nuts upon his glebe.[6] As in duty bound in a year of great abundance he sent a small picking to grace the table of His Majesty King George III at a time when he was taking the waters at Tunbridge Wells. The King after finishing them off with the second bottle of claret commanded with great emphasis and no doubt some lack of clear sibilation "send

---

[6] *The Reverend Samuel Cobb, Rector of Ightham. See guide to Kent County archives, 1958 p 209.*

me some more of Cobb's nuts" and the name thus stuck. As to the Filberts could full beard over the years have become contracted? A modern German name is Lambert snuss - nothing to do with Lambert the hybridizer, the propagator of the Kent Cob, but derived from Langbart syn Longbeard or long husk. According to Koch, Longobards or Lombards (long-bearded traders) brought the nuts from Lombardy over the Alps as they traded with the spreading Holy Roman Empire. Yet again, could they be St. Philberts nuts ripening on 22nd August, St Philbert's day? At a first glance this seems unlikely as the 22nd of August is a week or more too early to start picking, at any rate in Kent; but perhaps not if you give the cultivator back the days of which his ancestors were robbed in 1752 when the Gregorian (new style) calendar was adopted in this country, and it would not be unusual to be picking nuts on the 3rd of September for the early market.[7]

The Folklore

Corylus Avellana is said to be an emblem of fruitfulness in marriage. In northern countries it is considered to be a lightening plant and its wands or rods to be of use as a charm against witches and as bidding rods in the hands of authority. In Norse mythology the plant is sacred to Thor, the God of Thunder. The use of a forked branch or twig of hazel for water divining is well known but no scientific reason for this quality can be given, nor can it be said with any confidence that the quality is in the

[7] *Calendar (new style) Act 1750.*

fork rather than in the holder of the ends, as the rod twists and dips over the underground water source. Anne Pratt even credits it with the further magic of detecting underground minerals, back to very early days in Aquiola's time in this country and in the time of the prophet Hosea for the Israelites.[8] Maybe we must settle by accepting that both hazel and certain but not all holders share the magic between them.

The Chaos of the Names

The most comprehensive written work on Corylus is *Die Haselnuss* by Goesche produced in Berlin in 1887, containing detailed descriptions with life-sized plain plates of the different varieties.[9] It seems probable that save as sports from existing varieties or from accidental seedlings few additional varieties have been produced since that date and many have passed out of cultivation. The proliferation of named varieties seems to have begun at the beginning of the 19th century, and to have been in its heyday between 1820 and 1875. The Royal Horticultural Society Library contains the first and second editions of *Fruits Grown in the Experimental Gardens in 1826 and 1831*.[10] In both editions are long lists of varieties of the Avellana group, well over 30 in each. Looking critically at these lists it does seem that they well illustrate the confusion into which the naming of nuts had fallen. Much of this may have been due to slight differences

---

[8] *Hosea IV, verse 12.*
[9] *Was this work destroyed during the 1939-45 war? There is no trace of it now.*
[10] *At their Headquarters in Vincent Square, London SW1.*

within one variety when grown in the soil and local climate of say, Kent, Herefordshire and Furness in Lancashire and in such event acquiring different names in each locality. The lists seem to be inflated by differences in the local names for similar if not identical varieties, e.g. Peasants Prolific - Glasgow Prolific - Dwarf Prolific, as a case in point in the 1826 list. Again in addition, Northampton Prolific - Pearsons Prolific and Porimley in that of 1831. If one applies the same treatment to Lambert varieties and also eliminate those which would have been of interest to a foreign grower only, we find the list reduced to a manageable residue. Working from the Horticultural Society lists one can begin the 19th century with the following:

    Allesby
    Blue shelled filbert
    Bond nut
    Burn nut
    Lamberts cob
    Cosford cob
    Frizzled filbert
    Jevons seedlings
    Sir John Ambury's cob
    Toker
    Wrotham Park

Though it is by no means free from argument it is tenable that amongst these the parents of the improved varieties if indeed they really are improvements, are to be found. Just 100 years after the Royal Horticultural Society lists L. B. Bagnell of the East Malling Research Station lists the following varieties of Cobs and Filberts as grown in England.[11]

Cobnuts

Cosford cob; syn Miss Young's thin shelled nut
Webbs prize Cob
Pearsons prolific; syn Dwarf or Northampton prolific
Prolific
Cannonball
Duchess of Edinburgh, Dale of Edinburgh, Marquis of Lorne

Filberts

White Filbert; syn Avellana Blanche Langue
Red Filbert; syn Avellana Rouge Langue
Lamberts Filbert; syn Kent Cob
Prolific
Princess Royal
The Shap
Garibaldi
Daviana[12]
Webbs Prize[13]
La Bergeri

Save for Pearsons Prolific Group, and the Webb varieties, all are identifiable with Loudon's classification.

[11] *Fruit growing: L B Bagnell, pp 223.*
[12] *Appears closely allied to Cosford; a thicker shell but is it really a filbert?*
[13] *Webbs Prize appears in both lists but in Bagnell's description it appears only as a filbert. Maybe Webb's cob suffered in its name the same fate as did Lambert's filbert.*

The Development of Varieties

The first we know of this is a reference in the writings of a mid-seventeenth century herbalist Casper Bauhin of Lyons, who in 1623 refers to the Red and White filberts the long red and white nuts from Avellino and one other which he named Avellina Major Lugdunensis - the big nut of Lyons. Could that have been a precursor of the variety Geant de Halle, probably the largest of the Filberts raised by C.G. Buttner of Halle in 1778? Whether or not this be so it seems a logical progression by Avellina to have travelled over the years from the shores of the Black Sea through Greece to Campania thence by a small step across the water and up the Rhone to Lyons. There is nothing further worthy of comment until the early part of the 19th century when, in 1812 Brookshaw in "Pomona Britannica" lists 8 varieties. In 1816 the Cosford cob was marketed having been propagated by a nurseryman in the Ipswich area, doubtless having been first raised in the Hundred of Cosford in the near vicinity and not unlikely by that Miss Young after whom it was first named. Lambert of Goudhurst, Kent was, as we have seen, the next to produce a viable commercial variety which from 1830 became the most often planted in the county and which by its generally accepted name of Kent cob forms a major part of those plantations which still survive. This in essence was a development from Tubulosa and unlike Cosford, which is partially open in the husk and round in the nut whatever its name implies is most certainly a true filbert and let there be no mistake about that. In this country throughout the middle years of the century Richard Webb of Chilcot near Reading was the leading hybridizer and producer of Corylus varieties. He was an eccentric with a large house and a garden of 11 acres, walled to a height of 8ft most of which was devoted to the nursing and raising of seedling nuts.[14] His house so it is said was guarded by several bloodhounds and his garden protected from the birds by 40 cats. Apart from his nut bushes his garden contained a monument to alcohol under which it is said that in a moment of temperance he buried all the choicest wines in his cellar.[15] So says Bunyard but in his obituary notice in the Gardener's Chronicle of August 1877 the hounds are said to have been mastiffs and the cats "of various nationalities" but only "a score or more". To all of which he was devoted. Maybe Bunyard included the kittens. Bunyard refers to him as Thomas but the Ministry of Agriculture Bulletin No. 106 attributes the varieties subsequently named to Richard.

Research at the Royal Horticultural Society Library leads one to suppose that Bunyard's Thomas was a myth and that only Richard raised the nuts. It is unfortunate that he left no documentary record of his work so we do not know the parentage of his varieties and all that can be said is that he raised a large number of seedlings, the best of which were propagated and brought to the market by his son-in-law T.O. Cooper of Reading.

Whether it was Webb or Cooper who had the taste for high-sounding names for the successful varieties we cannot say but the Duke and the Duchess of Edinburgh, the Marquis of Lorne, Garibaldi and Webb's Prize were five of the best to come from this stable, the first-named winning a Royal Horticultural Society 1st Class certificate

---

[14] *At any reasonable planting distance an eleven acre walled garden could easily have contained 2000 bushes.*
[15] *Perhaps a 19th. century euphemism for a fit of alcoholic remorse.*

when exhibited in 1883.

Pearson and Co of Nottingham appeared to have been responsible for Pearson's Prolific which it is said was developed by them from a seedling brought back from Labrador by a friend. La Bergeri, a development from the Frizzled nut was a later arrival, being raised by Jacob Mackoy of Liege in the mid 1860s.

Varieties from the Merrimans plantation. Clockwise from upper left: Prolific, Cosford, Pearson's Prolific, White Lambert, Frizzled Filbert.

The weight of authority dating the introduction and planting of Lambert's filbert as the most common nut in Kent at 1830 throws considerable doubt on the authenticity of the story of George III and the Reverend Cobb, since the monarch died a year before the planting of Lambert's filbert began. Whatever our loyalty to our own local legend may be one must have reservations to make about it as the date is only consistent with the Rev'd gentleman tending on his glebe one of the earlier varieties, Cosford perhaps would just fit the bill. It is too good a story to discard entirely and it certainly goes some way to explain the growth in the popularity of Cobbs just at that time, if it is to be believed.

The Economics and Distribution

Corylus is a labour intensive crop and not one that anyone would plant today for profit. However it has possibilities as a garden or orchard tree. It is doubtful whether any commercial plantations have been made since 1930. Statistics available show a commercial acreage in Kent of 3300 acres in 1913 and 6300 by 1917[16] In a later advisory leaflet the figures for 1935 are given as 2056 and in 1957 down to 943. [17] Since then more and more acres have been grubbed to make way for more profitable crops or left untended and unharvested for lack of labour. If you could find 250 acres in cultivation under nuts today that would be a lot.

So when nuts were profitable they provided a useful cash crop from which the commercial raiser could keep his workforce employed between the end of the cereal harvest and the time when the potatoes and other root crops were ready for lifting, but that goes back to the turn of the century. In 1913 the price to the grower averaged four pence per pound; by the end of the 1914/18 war it had doubled and by 1939 had doubled again. Since then as the

---

[16] *Ministry of Agriculture Bulletin No.106.*
[17] *Ministry of Agriculture advisory leaflet No. 4001966.*

supplies to the market have steadily diminished and as the cost in production and wages has increased the price has continued to rise until in Sept 1982 the early pickings were bringing home 35-40 new pence per pound. Out of that in theory the grower has to meet a labour charge arrived at as follows:

Pruning	15 mins
Wanning	15 mins
Spatting	10 mins
Brutting	5 mins (if carried out)
Picking	15 mins
Packing	5 mins
TOTAL.	1 hr 5 mins.

Assuming a density of 197 trees per acre each acre absorbs 213 hours or 28 working days of 7.5 hours which at £15 per day gives an outlay on wages of £420.

In olden days of low labour costs when nuts were grown under clean culture and not a weed or a blade of grass was allowed to grow between the rows a yield of over 2 tons per acre was said not to be unusual.[18] Under conditions as they are today the crop can vary from almost a nothing to half a ton! If a grower can average a return of six hundredweight from the acre he is doing well. In other words the grower must content himself with a gross return of £268 per acre on average which is absurd; there still remains to be taken into account the cost of packing

---

[18] *The degree of cleanliness and tonnage yields could well be facts that in stories told to me by the oldest inhabitants of the parish were prone to grow in the telling.*

materials, marketing expenses, depreciation on mechanized implements to say nothing of interest on capital sunk in the purchase of the land itself. Small wonder that "Kent cobs" have commercially long since ceased to be a viable proposition and are now an anachronism. However, be that as it may though they may no longer be of interest to the farmer, to the private grower with perhaps an acre so, if he can make use of his own labour and that of his wife and of any willing family or friends, Corylus can still contribute to his overheads involved in maintaining a country home and garden and provide a source of interest and enjoyment throughout the year as well as a great deal of health promoting exercise. I am afraid that those of us who can look upon their nut crop in this light are an ever-decreasing minority and that in another ten years' time there will be no longer any nuts to go to market. It is that thought that encouraged me, having tended my own 200 trees for so long to research some of the history of the species and then to record my experiences with my own small patch for whatever interest it may be to future generations.

The Culture

The literature tells us that nut trees will grow anywhere, that indeed is true, but it is also true that if planted in soil which is too rich the trees will run to top growth wood; wood for bean poles and pea boughs but not so good for the production of nuts. The tree is a great forager, putting out roots to a considerable distance laterally in search of sustenance, but not downwards in the way a taller growing tree would do in order to maintain its anchorage.

Consequently it can find a good living and bear well on sandy and gravelly soils where other fruits would underperform their potential or fail. Hence it is that the major plantings of Kent cobs were found on the ragstone ridge of the lower greensand belt and immediately adjacent thereto in the area between Sevenoaks and Maidstone, with but few in other parts of Kent. Outside of the county they are found in Herefordshire, on the Cotswold slopes and in Furness.[19]

All varieties are slow to mature, and could according to the old growers be expected to produce 5lb of nuts per tree after 7 years growth subsequently rising to 10lb and maintaining that figure from the 12th year onwards with a profitable life expectancy of 150 years at least. Since a well-cared for tree can be expected to have a spread of 12ft or more when fully grown the usual planting distance was 15ft in a square plant giving 197 trees to the acre.

The slow growth and what might in the early years be considered to be a wide spacing with consequent negative land use in terms of return on capital led in many cases to the practice of interplanting with standard apples, mainly Bramleys on a vigorous stock.[20] In this way some return was obtained in earlier years. How sound the practice really was is hard to say and it is probably impossible to set a general rule. If the growers object was to establish a nut plantation then it had to be borne in mind that one thing that cobs dislike beyond all else is shade and with it drip and damp. Hence it is imperative that the additional

---

[19] *Planted for coppice wood for the furnaces of the local iron industry.*
[20] *It is worthy of note that in the nut planting era the dwarf pyramid form of apple had not been developed, the planting of cordons was a garden venture only and Malling was only a twinkle in the fruit-grower's eye.*

planting be taken out as soon as it has spread into or over the nuts. In many cases that could be before the cost of overplanting had been fully recovered and the temptation was to carry the apples for a little longer whenever the question arose. If overcrowding and poor performance over the years by both was to be avoided either the cobs or the apples should have been grubbed certainly by the tenth year from planting. It was fatal to expect to obtain the best of both worlds.

A possible alternative and one of which I can see traces of adoption in my own plantation today, was to interplant with redcurrants or raspberries which would reach the end of their natural life at just about the time when nuts were reaching their maturity. I have found descendants of these and occasionally gooseberries too coming up in the wild parts of my woodland wherever sufficient light penetrates the foliage of the overgrowing silver birch and sycamore to germinate long dormant seed. Indeed I have rescued several of the redcurrant seedlings from time to time and replanted them in the soft fruit garden area where they are, if left alone, capable at the end of a season of reaching a height of 5ft with a similar spread of the branches. They produce a good currant and yield well given protection from the birds when in bud and when ripening.

One does not have to look around very far today to find evidence of the greedy grower who left his apples in, where his apples trees have grown up to their full height beyond regulation and the reach of ladders and the crop is left to fall and provide a feast for the blackbirds when the first frosts come in. In the meantime the nuts among which they were originally planted have gone up with the apples. Bracken and brambles have crept in and such a dense tangle exists that what few nuts fall are not worth the labour of picking up. Indeed a neglected plantation such as this is a pathetic sight to see. One can only think that where this has been allowed to happen the quality of the land is such that it does not justify the cost of grubbing out and replanting with a more valuable crop. Under the clean culture system appropriate to the days when the agricultural wage was as low as 12/6d. per week the recollection of one or two of the oldest inhabitants of my acquaintance was that one man working full-time throughout the year could maintain 5 acres of nut bushes but that additional labour had to be brought in at picking time.

The Geology

I have spent a little time trying to discover what if any relation there may be in my own particular area, being that part of the lower greensand ridge lying within the confines of the parishes of Ightham, Plaxtol, Shipbourne, Seal Chart and Mereworth, between the planting of Kent cobs and the local geology. One fact is fairly plain, and that is that no plantations were extensively made in any areas in which a more valuable crop could be expected to flourish. Insight into this can easily be obtained if one goes to any high point in the vicinity of Crowhurst with an open aspect to the east and looks north east and south east onto the Valley of the Bourne and spies out the number of Oasts on the farms occupying the bottom and lower slopes of the valley. On a clear day one can count up to 20. Then looking at the geological map of the area one can see at once that these are all on farms lying in the alluvial valley.

The soil on the earliest of the lower greensand formations, the Hythe beds has enough in it to encourage the planting of hops or of hop on stocks of medium vigour. Thus one finds that the younger formations, the Folkstone and Sandgate beds with their lighter sandy soils were left to the nut growers who in the early part of the 19th century might otherwise have allowed such relatively unprofitable land to go to waste.

That I think is an established trend though not a rule. There are exceptions, any cobs growing in the vicinity of Mereworth for instance are planted on a subsoil of Hythe beds and I have found evidence of plantations as far into the Wealden clay as Paddock Wood. The only indisputable conclusion that I can draw is that there is a relationship, although a tenuous one.

If one takes my own immediate area at the time of the 1938 6″ Ordinance Survey as being that lying within the triangle formed by the Coach Road, Ismays Road and Sandy Lane it is clear that out of 17.5 acres then shown on the map only 2.5 acres remain planted today with the original trees and receive some limited cultural attention from year to year. The map shows an estimate for the area of cobnut plantations as they may have been in the Parish of Ightham in the 1930s. If the whole acreage of the Parish be 2610 as thereon stated it would be generous to trace within Ightham and Ivy Hatch a total plant of 875 acres.[21] In the adjoining Parishes of Plaxtol, Seal, Mereworth and Borough Green the planting was not so dense, perhaps another 1000/1250 acres. This goes a fair way towards meeting the Ministry's figure of 2056 as given for 1937. It

---

[21] *See Appendix 1.*

is certainly clear that by 1930, save in our contiguous Parishes the main earlier plantings had been grubbed up accounting for the reduction of the Ministry's figure of 7300 acres given for 1913.

One is tempted to say that the gradual demise of the cob nut as a commercial proposition is partly attributable to the success of the East Malling Research Establishment, Long Ashton and the like in developing new improved varieties of hard fruits, raspberries, strawberries and other produce acceptable to the market, all particularly suited to our particular soils and environments, thus rendering the sandy layers of the lower greensand suitable for conversion to less labour intensive crops and bit by bit confining the cobs to the area of Ightham and its adjoining Parishes.[22]

Propagation and Development

"Kent cobs" will not come true from seed; to maintain a strain vegetative propagation is necessary.[23] This is the accepted commercial method though I can see no reason why in special cases some form of grafting should not be attempted. In the nurseries the layers were pegged down from the parent tree in October and left for 18 months before they were lined out in rows. After 12 months the whip is shortened to form the leg on which the bush is to develop, cutting back to a height of 2 - 3ft.

[22] *See Appendix 2*
[23] *In this respect they are like the date palms of Arabia.*

Well pruned nut bushes are the reward for long hours of work

At this stage 10 years to fruit bearing seems a long time. I believe a year may be saved by taking off more growth coming from below ground level which would otherwise be layered and whenever possible treating them as rooted cuttings and lining out straight away, cutting back to form the leg in 12 months. The leg once formed, all buds save three facing in different directions are rubbed out. The retained buds are allowed to push out and in the spring of the following year the operation is repeated so that now 9 buds are pushing out and yet again in a year's time 27 branches are coming into existence and the framework of a tree has been established which now has to be moved to its permanent site. Give it a year to settle down and nuts should begin to appear. The open conventional champagne glass shape of bush has the advantage of allowing the maximum penetration of both light and air into the centre, thus encouraging the production of the short twiggy form of growth essential to carry the female flowers; and the maintenance of this shape keeps the nuts therein at a height which is practicable for the pickers if the harvest is to be gathered off the trees in the early stage of ripening.

I do not put this forward as the best or only method. However I have always adhered to it and have found it satisfactory though it does involve a lot of work in the pruning months. Others do adopt and may well derive other benefits from the champagne flute rather than the open glass allowing the trees to go up to their natural height while constricting their lateral spread. This method postulates growing for the later market when the nuts have fully ripened to maturity and fall or are shaken to the ground, there to be picked up rather than down. The choice is a matter of which method suits the grower's pocket and the pickers back best. With judgment coloured by a preference for the open glass method, I would advocate that the heavy pruning necessary to maintain this shape promotes the production of a large nut and of nuts in larger clusters and that by growing for the earlier market one steers clear of the risk of running into competition with the Barcelona nuts when they arrive in October and November.[24] [25] Possibly, too, there is some

[24] *With the exception of Prolific the descriptions of varieties by others in all cases refer to clusters of nuts in two and three. With me Cosford conforms to this rule more or less but it is nothing to find eight or more in a cluster of our Lamberts or La Bergeri. In 1983 a cluster of 16 Lamberts was found.*
[25] *In 1937 4520 tons of Barcelona nuts were imported. At that time the home-grown crop averaged 1950 tons. Ministry of Agriculture Advisory Leaflet No. 400; 1966.*

advantage in having the productive wood at a low height where it can benefit from any surrounding shelter belt available thus obtaining some protection against damage to the male catkin from the winter gales of January and February when the pollen is approaching the stage of viability rather than have it swaying about on high and being carried away in all the winds that blow.

A compromise, an idea which has only been brought to my attention recently and which I wish I had thought of for myself many years ago may well be to take one limb of each bush in say every third row and allow one upward growing new wand from the topmost node to grow on and cut back after 3ft of growth allowing the side buds to grow out at the top, thus in effect forming a catkin bearing umbrella, spaced in such a way that from whichever quarter the wind may blow, and our south-westerlies can easily veer and stay in a northerly of easterly quarter for many days in the early part of the year, you have a satisfactory fall and drift of pollen over all your rows.

Manurial Requirements

Corylus may ruin you with labour charges but certainly will not break you at the bank with payments for artificials. A little nitrogen goes a long way. A little more will go too far. In the old days of clean culture some nitrogenous dressings were applied. Today when 10 cwt to the acre is an excellent yield from trees grown in grass very little need be done. Possibly following a year which produced an exceptionally heavy crop a light dressing of slow-acting nitrogen might be useful and perhaps an inexpensive form of phosphorus could help build up the young trees at the time of planting. I very much doubt the wisdom of formulating any general rule, so much depends on the individual grower's site and soil. For my own trees my experience is that a policy of leave well alone is best That by cutting back the grass and other growth twice during the growing season, allowing the mowings and likewise the smaller prunings of March and April to rot back into the soil one is probably giving the tree sufficient nourishment to keep it healthy without stimulating it into too vigorous leaf at the expense of the production of nut-bearing growth. I would go as far as to say that if both time and pocket permitted a light dressing of lime in every fifth year can do no harm and that so far as any ashes from a wood burning stove are available or for that matter bonfire ash before the weather has leached the value out of it were to be broadcast over and around the boles it would be putting to profitable use what otherwise might be condemned as rubbish.

Pruning

In addition to what has already been written in the section dealing with propagation and development where the methods of pruning to establish the framework and shape of the tree or bush have been considered, seasonal pruning is also necessary to maintain both shape and thriftiness once the trees have become established. Such seasonal work falls into three categories.

First, in the autumn, as soon as the leaves have fallen, the wands formed by the new season's growth are removed with any similar growth springing from the lower 2 - 3ft of the framework. Secondly, in the spring as soon as the catkins have begun to wither and fall, top pruning and general shortening of all twiggy growth and the removal of inward-growing branches springing from the main stems has to be attended to. Lastly, in July and early August, if it is found that the centres of the bushes are becoming choked with new growth obstructing the penetration of light and air to the ripening fruit and to the new wood to be retained to bear the following years crop, the inward growing new growth may be broken and left hanging a fists width from its base an operation known locally as "brutting".

It is a fair generalization to say that Corylus nuts are born on the top three feet of each branch. If the champagne flute shape is chosen a great deal of spring pruning over the top of the tree becomes impossible and unnecessary and the tendency to throw wands is reduced.

March is the time for Fred Broad to start pruning; to preserve the shape of the tree and to keep the nut bearing wood within the reach of the pickers.

As an example of this form of culture one can well take a look at the nut walk in the garden at Sissinghurst Castle, where trees at least 15ft high have been underplanted with mixed polyanthus. In springtime and before the leafing out of the overhead foliage forms too dense a canopy for the light to come through the effect is of a multi-coloured carpet. However the nuts themselves come at a height of 12 -15ft from the ground and can only be picked up in a harvested state. In this instance, since the plantation is hardly a commercial one, it is none the worse for that and the effect in springtime of the glowing catkin followed by bursting leaf bud with the vivid underplant is more than ample justification.

Whichever method of pruning is adopted the winter care when the "wanning" (as it is always referred to in my locality) is undertaken, is of the first importance. This is a tiresome process, not only is the object to get rid of the summer's vigorous upward growing pale, almost hazel coloured wands coming from the bole and branches but also to rid the tree of the smaller sucker growth which spring up all around it.

I recall many years ago an account given me by a very prominent fruit-grower in the area who well recalled the days of clean culture when his trees were mostly still growing on the original legs from which they had been trained. His rules were, first, never to permit the use of a knife of any sort; every growth removed had to be broken out of its base so as to avoid stimulating the surrounding basal buds into growth; next, he expected his workers to take mattocks and with the broad end to go round the base of each tree and sever the small surface clinging roots which throw up the smaller sucker growths and pull these right out. I must confess that it is many years since any of my bushes have seen the sharp end of a mattock, though I do recall a dear old friend, who helped me in the garden in the immediate post-war years, carefully grubbing around each tree and being most insistent that if this was not done, all the nuts would go to the roots instead of to the branches where they ought to be. In support of his argument he used to produce handfuls of nutshells mostly with a hole nibbled out on one side typical of the way a mouse would deal with them, which he brought up out of the soil with his mattock head. All very well at the time but then my friend was a unique character whose rate for the job was one shilling per hour and he would take no more for fear of affecting his pension!

Certainly if the flute method be adopted the labour cost of this winter wanning is substantially reduced. The pruning over the top ceases to be a charge and there is a reduction in the picking cost, but against this has to be set the loss in size of the nuts and of the number in the cluster to say nothing of some loss from vermin.

Whatever one's favourite method may be one thing is certain; it must be accepted that no worthwhile growth can be retained or indeed obtained unless plenty of light is allowed to penetrate to the centre of the bush. Accordingly if the open champagne glass shape is chosen that must be the first objective of the spring pruning; the second must be to keep the growth of the tree within reasonable bounds laterally, and thirdly to promote the production of nut-bearing wood on that three feet of every branch as is within comfortable reach of the picker.

If this spring pruning over the top is adequately carried out, the August brutting operation should not be necessary, indeed I have never found it so. The timing of pruning operations is very much affected by seasonal influences. If it is possible to begin the wanning as the leaves come down and finish with it by Christmas that would be an ideal state of affairs; but autumn is a busy time all round the garden and woods and the wanning seldom receives the priority that a Christmas finish would require.

When to start the spring pruning is again a matter of what first the season and then the weather will permit. Given a good show of male catkin well distributed throughout the plantation one can begin this part of the years' work as soon as the trees emerge from dormancy but if pruning early it is necessary to be selective in view of the way one variety may differ from another in response to the very small increase in daylight hours in January.[26] If the male catkin is sparse it is best to defer pruning until all the pollen has been shed and then one can move from tree to tree irrespective of variety.

---

[26] *In 1983 La Bergeri was beginning to show the yellow glow of pollen on the 6th. of January*

Inward growing new wood is removed to allow light into the centre of the tree.

It is a great temptation when dealing with last season's whippy growth so far as it arises from the nodes of the branches to cut back to the top most female flower as on such growth there may be many. This is a mistake; the whole should be broken out because although such female flower may develop the nutkins will be borne well above the shade of the leaf and at the critical stage in their development will be exposed to the full glare of the mid-summer sun. Many will fail to mature and finish up as little burnt up under-developed remains. These are troublesome at picking time when in order to preserve the quality of the sample they have to be picked out; a very tedious and thumb-ache making business. In recent years I have found that on the better trained trees more and more buds and fruit appear at every node of each branch. I have often wondered whether one would get the same size of crop by taking off every bit of old growth all the way up and over the top of each node allowing the nodal buds alone to develop. That is something I would certainly try on some of the trees if I had another 10 years in which to experiment.

Diseases

Considering the amount of cutting, breaking out and general hacking about that goes on in every well-regulated nut plantation over the years it is hard to think of any form of culture more resistant to disease than Kent cobs. True, from time to time some form of virus sets in leading to die back of the twiggy growth and even to whole branches but in my experience this does not amount to a serious scourge and it is easy to train in replacement growths in case of need. I do however relate the fact that nearly all my own trees are now growing on a stool from which new branches have been trained, rather than on their original single leg, to the possibility that some infection may have destroyed the original leg and framework though overgrowth and light deprivation may also have been a cause.

There are brown rots and bud rots present from time to time doing some damage to the buds and nuts but I have not found the extent of these to be serious at any time. [27] [28]

[27] *Monilinia Fructigena.*
[28] *Glocosporium.*

Old dead wood is removed with a saw and if need be a new wand is trained in as a replacement.

An alternative possibility, and in my view a more acceptable explanation of die back, maybe that somewhere along the line of their long life-time, (most of my trees must be 150 years old) they have been neglected and allowed to go up in height to 15ft or more in such a way that the new growth, creating a dense area of shade and damp and in the process drawing away the nourishment from the original framework, allowed decay to set in.

The Pests: Insects

There is, it is said, a mite which attacks the twigs causing them to dry out and wither. [29] I have no first-hand

---

[29] *Phytophus Avellanae.*

experience of it. Another like it within the lengthening catkin or swelling leaf bud, usually referred to as the gall mite, I have found more common. [30] In effect it looks very like a relative to the big bud mite on blackcurrants, but has not the harmful capacity to host the virus of reversion. The nut gall weevil was a serious problem in the immediate post war years (as was the apple blossom weevil) laying its egg amongst the whiskers of the female flowers one by one as they opened. [31] These hatched into a small white grub which developed within the chosen individual nut Unlike the activities of the apple blossom weevil this grub did not abort the whole process of development; Affected nuts swelled to their usual size but within the shell the weevil grew fatter and stronger and eventually consumed the whole milky substance which would otherwise have developed into the nut. At that stage when perhaps a centimetre in length its jaws were sufficiently strong for it to chew through the shell and then in a leathery state, drop to the ground to pupate and begin the life cycle all over again. The emerging grub left evidence of its activities in the form of a small round black hole in the centre of the nut indicating its passage into the open world.

These black holed nuts used to be a nuisance when picking as some would get into the pickers bag and a good deal of time and trouble had to be taken sorting and turning to get rid of every last one. The nuts however much they were turned or shaken, had a remarkable ability for hiding the little black holes on the underside! Before the era of modern pesticides the treatment for this was to dust the trees with arsenate of lead in March. Now I do

[30] *Ereophes Avellanae.*
[31] *Balaninus Nucus.*

nothing as it is many years since I have seen any damage of this sort on my own trees. I find it difficult to give a sure and certain reason for this though I suspect that I have been the beneficiary of the big clean up in orchards of all kinds when DDT first became available to the commercial fruit-grower. That certainly put paid to the apple blossom weevil. In addition it is possible that my method of cutting the grass and letting it lie where it falls may have had, as it heated and decayed, a suffocating effect upon the grub as it was going through the stage of its life preparatory to pupation.

There is sometimes evidence of pest damage to the tender young leaves. A search for the culprit has never been very successful though from time to time I have found a bright green shield shaped creature with a typical weevil's snout about the size of a little fingernail. This has been welcome to the limited leaf damage which it has caused as it is an attractive and interesting creature in itself. No less interesting in its way, though quite calamitous, was an event which occurred in one year in the late 1940s. At that time the area lying under the flank of Raspit Hill to the north west of Merrimans was in a post-war neglected state, in the main covered with bramble patches and overgrown untended Bramley apple trees. On a day in May as a light north west wind blew down the hill and over the derelict area onto my nuts it was my fate to watch a quite remarkable hatch of winter moth caterpillars on the old apples.[32] Putting up their slender silken threads they became airborne in their thousands and drifted down on to my nuts just coming into

[32] *Probably Tortrix Viridana; the caterpillars known locally as 'loopers'.*

leaf. By noon the next day defoliation was complete. Subsequently there was some leaf recovery but not a nut was produced and the debilitating effect on the trees persisted for another year.

The Pests: Larger Animals

The first of the animal pests is the grey squirrel.[33] In this woodland area the squirrel population is fairly constant and it follows that the nuts they take do not vary in weight much from year to year. In a poor year one regrets the loss of every pound of nuts, in a good one the same loss is scarcely noticeable. It is, I believe, right to adopt a philosophic attitude to the grey. Though his capacity for mischief in the garden is boundless and the damage he does to early nesting birds and their eggs is beyond belief, even though, should you rob him of his tail you are left with nothing other than an unbalanced tree rat, it is best to pay one's squirrel tax by year and forget it while being grateful for the interest and grace his erratic and seemingly inconsequential movements lend to the garden scene. It is said he robs you of nuts, buries them, and then forgets where they are when he is hungry. I am not convinced. I have never, when digging around the garden come across a squirrel hoard of harvested nuts. Furthermore he always takes the small wild nuts in the hedgerows to which he is welcome before he starts on the heavier cultivated crop. If he is going to take them away

---

[33] *Within the Parish Ightham is to be found a breed of Squirrel with pure white coats, not just a winter coat nor a true albino. Such whites I have seen on several occasions; leucistic is the word for them.*

up to his drey every ounce of weight is to him what a pound would be to you or me.

After the grey squirrel come an infinite variety of small rodents of which the long-tailed fieldmouse is the one which is the most common here. He and his smaller relatives have the capacity to accumulate quite substantial stores of de-husked and well-polished nuts against the coming of winter. If you can find one of these you can be sure of an excellent sample for the house. The small creatures know very well the difference between a good nut and a bad or decaying one and will never waste energy laying by the latter. I think that it was in the autumn of our second year at Merrimans that we tried to be clever and to pick a small crop of nuts as early as possible but to save them for marketing later on in October. If I recall correctly that year we only picked perhaps 300 lb. and all of these were stored in the loft as it then was over the garage and in bulk amounted to two tea chests full. On returning from a September holiday we inspected the two chests, and to our surprise found that the contents had gone down by half. To our further surprise we found that the half remaining consisted entirely of husks and that every last nut had vanished. Clearly the work of small rodents as one or two caches were found on the brick ledges underneath the eaves of the loft. But how the operation was carried out remains a mystery even today. Our only theory is that mice can and do adopt the same technique with cob nuts that a pair of rats employ to rob a hen's nest. One mouse clasping a nut between its forepaws while a companion takes it by the tail and drags it out of the chest; but what height of a wooden perpendicular wall could a healthy mouse scale dragging a partner by the tail behind it?

Certainly a lift of 18 inches would then have been required to clear the rim of the chest once the level of nuts had shrunk by that amount from the top.

In the world of birds the nut hatch takes its share. Even though this bird seems to have increased in numbers quite considerably in recent years, whatever he takes is minimal and well worth the pleasure of his colourful company and cheerful piping in the early months of the year. The occasional coven of mischievous rooks can do far more damage to the crop if it attacks them in the days before ripening when the shell is still soft.

When considering pests it would be a mistake to ignore the activity of rascally small boys and of gypsies. Either of these if of local stock and familiar with the habit of growth of Corylus can strip a bush by running his hands up either side of a branch just as well in the dark as in the daytime. In this way on several occasions I have lost most of the crop from those trees remote from the house and adjacent to the Coach Road.

Pollination

Corylus nuts are by nature self-fertile and cross pollination is not essential if the nuts are to develop.[34] However, self-fertile or not some variation of the varieties within the plantation is desirable. A surrounding hedge of the common wild hazel is an excellent wind break but can also provide pollen from its own natural catkins in a bad year for the cultivated nut and fertilize the nutkins almost

---

[34] Editor's note. Later research has shown that not all varieties of Corylus, including Lambert's Filbert, are self-fertile.

as well. What is true of the pollen from the hedgerow nuts is also true of all the varieties of nuts. To have a mixed plant, with slight difference in the dates on which the catkins and nutkins mature, protects Kent cobs from the failure of the nutkin to appear before the pollen has been shed and become exhausted. Lamberts filbert is particularly vulnerable in this way, as its catkin can in a mild January develop in a week, while the wiser female flowers hold back in the certain knowledge of hard and windy weather still to come.

The pollination process begins with the turn of the year. In most years, if one looks for it, one can then find traces of the lengthening, opening and appearance of the yellow tinge at the end of some of the catkins. By the end of January the catkin reaches its full length on Lamberts, and some female flowers should be showing. From there on one looks for an afternoon with a light drying breeze and warm sunshine, a temperature of 50°F is ideal for the pollen to become viable, and drift away in clouds of gold, in value at any rate if rather a pale gold in colour. In any ordinary year one can hope for one or two such afternoons in February. That given, one can rest assured of a reasonable crop.

Needless to say such ideal conditions are far from happening every year, usually the operation has to be spread over more afternoons than one and on briefer periods of time within the day. On certain days one can find that the pollen will fly for just for a few minutes at a time. However, provided the nutkin is in a receptive state, that is to say with anthers well spread and dry, one good drift of pollen can ensure the crop in a matter of moments.

In winter the nut plantation is a bleak place; but even in the snows of January there is a tinge of yellow as the catkins swell.

The principal cause of failure to pollenate properly is failure of either male or female to appear in sufficient quantities at the right time or indeed at all. It is said that heavy cropping can induce a tendency towards a biennial habit of bearing. Maybe my crops have not been heavy enough but I have never found it so. Given a sparse spread of male flower in certain years we have, on what has seemed a suitable day, taken a broom stick down the rows tap-tap-tapping the bushes as we pass and thus liberating any latent pollen, but I am not convinced that this is really necessary or beneficial. It may well be better to rely on the more natural liberation of the pollen over a period. It is always surprising how, even well on into March when the catkins appear to have browned right off and to be ready to drop, much dust will still fly with a little agitation on a warm afternoon. Weather conditions do not affect Corylus as much as one might expect. Both catkin and nutkin are remarkably hardy. The nutkin, when it appears, seems almost indestructible and will certainly survive ten degrees of frost and the catkin, unless fully opened, will do the same; but if cold be coupled with high winds and wet conditions when the catkins are open the pollen if it moves at all can be blown up and away to the next Parish, and if it fails to move can consolidate into a yellow sticky mess. If that happens the nutkins must look to another source of pollen from a later variety for fertilization.

One expedient in such an event is to throw up any prunings lying about carrying undamaged catkin onto the tops of any bushes carrying none. As an additional safeguard against the loss of the male flowers on Lamberts filberts, whoever was responsible for my own original plant took steps to guard against it by mixing his varieties. Though I am unable to identify them all I am sure of the following which supplement the main planting of Lamberts filbert: Cosford cob, a prolific catkin producer whose catkins develop late and whose nutkins come later still, consequently in some years a light cropper in itself. Pearsons prolific also bears its catkins well and high, produces its nuts in large clusters though the nut itself is small. La Bergeri - the frizzled nut, produces catkins early and of inordinate length up to 4 inches and nutkins come late: again in itself a sparse cropper in some years but it should and I am sure often does pollenate from Pearsons prolific growing nearby. This is an interesting variety and I suspect that I should more accurately describe it as a La Bergeri type which may well be an ancestor of the true La Bergeri frizzled nut not developed until the 1860s.

Certainly of the nuts themselves there are two distinct forms, one with square shoulders and one more rounded at the base, otherwise they exactly conform to the description given by Bunyard but the husks do not, being far better described as "frothy" rather than frizzled and beautifully coloured from light green to hazel. A bunch or two of these nuts when just picked would enhance any still-life study of a bowl of fruit. Finally the White Lambert of the Barcelona group which can produce catkins in a year when no other tree does and produces them long and early.[35]

The Advancing Year

The process of leafing out begins as both fruit and growth buds swell and burst and the catkins begin to fall. In any normal year the plantation is well clad in green by the time that the apple blossom is in flower. It is always a race to finish the top pruning prior to bud burst. For safety sake it may well be wise to regard the end of the first week in May as the end of the pruning period. After that with the spring flow of sap at its height any further knife work is only done at the risk of doing more harm than good.

By the beginning of June the baby nuts begin to appear and by the end of the month it is possible to say with confidence what sort of crop there will be to harvest.

[35] *See Appendix 3 for drawings of catkin development in different varieties.*

By March the catkin has all browned off and the daffodils are showing their leaves: it will be another month before the leaf buds swell.

Mowing and Weeding

It is desirable, taking one's time from the browning off of the tips of the daffodil leaves to cut the grass through and across the rows and afterwards to apply a weed killer over and around the boles of the trees. The vigorous growth of June and July leaves the ground and the trees at their densest so by August if any trimming is to be done or any bracken growth slashed back this is the month in which to attend to it while a further onslaught with the mower on the grass and weed growth is desirable so as to maintain the morale of the pickers in September. There is nothing worse than having the lobe of one's ear stung by nettles when nut picking!

*By May the leaf buds are swollen and ready for the
"bud burst"*

In our early years though our lawn grass was cut with a
mower, the cutting through the nuts was done with a
scythe. Those were the days when the cost of our
particular labour was one shilling per hour. In 1950 we
acquired an Allen scythe with a 1.75 horsepower Jap
engine at a cost at that time of £50. After 2 years we
improved on this by putting it on a wide axle for greater
stability when cutting at an angle on a slope and by adding
a side cut. The latter was useful as it enabled the operator
to cut closely to the boles of the trees underneath the
overhanging branches. But as the years went by it became
a menace; guiding the machine with the side cut on was a
back wrenching affair particularly if the scythe snagged
upon an obstruction hidden in the long grass. The Allen
scythe, for all that, rendered valuable service for 25 years,
both to me and to others who borrowed it. It required the

bare minimum of attention and hardly ever asked for more. Left in a damp shed over the winter given a tank of clean fuel in the spring in 9 years out of 10 it would start after 2 or 3 pulls with the starting cord.[36] In 1973 the Allen went into retirement and was superseded by a rotary Hayter Osprey powered by a 7 horsepower Briggs & Stratton engine which was capable of driving a 21 inch cut through almost anything.

On the subject of weed control I agree with the experts who say that given care to apply on certain days only and the use of a hooded lance to avoid any drift to spray on to the lower leaves, the bushes themselves suffer no harm from the application of weedkillers though I am inclined to think that by killing off the grass from the immediate surround one may encourage rather more of the growth of the low whippy twigs arising from the underlying subsurface roots. I have applied SBK for a number of years and have found it satisfactory. Latterly I have turned over to Glyphosate. In the form of Tumbleweed this is expensive in retail quantities, but it certainly clears the surrounds of almost everything and it has a more lasting effect than SBK and operates right to the roots, even of nettles.[37]

The principal weeds with which we have to contend are Hogweed, Fools Parsley, thistles in many varieties, Rose Bay Willow herb, Bindweed, Black Briony and Hops. For the last of these I have as yet found no satisfactory control

[36] An Allen scythe is shown in Appendix 4. This is the narrow wheelbase version with the side cut fitted. It was also possible to fit a barrow on top which helped in bringing the harvested nuts back to the garage for packing.
[37] Editor's note. Although use of these chemicals was standard in the 1980s, SBK and Glyphosate are now only legal for garden use.

as also is the case with invasive bracken though it is a simple matter to pull it down and flatten it at picking time where it has become a nuisance.

By July the grass is waist high; taking the scythe through the plantation at this stage will ease the work of the pickers in September.

Picking, Packing and Marketing

We have found it useful to pick into hessian bags slung from the neck on tapes. In the late 40's, so far as hired labour was concerned, the rate of reward was as low as fourpence per lb. but this very quickly rose to a shilling and later in the new money to 10p. In the main, however, the picking, save in the case of a very heavy year, has been a joint enterprise greatly enjoyed by my wife and myself. Between us, and without undue effort, a weekend spent picking nuts could see us with upwards of 100 lb in the trays while during the weekday afternoons my wife and our lady who used to help up in the house could obtain that amount or more. I recall that in one bumper year our Florence turned in 90lb after a 2 hour afternoon stint. Normally, however, I would consider that any individual who averaged 15lb in

If the scythe is not used then access to the trees where the nuts are ready is extremely restricted not to say painful for the pickers.

an hour was doing very well but it is hardly right to lay down a norm as conditions of crops can vary so much from one year to the next.

We have found it useful to pick into hessian bags slung from the neck on tapes and not exceeding 12 inches in depth, thus not over-weighting oneself but leaving both hands free for gathering. We tip the nuts into the widest top barrow we have, so as to expose the greatest possible quantity of nuts for inspection, a turn or two will eliminate most of those bad, burned, or holey nuts so damaging to the quality demanded in the market place. We have two rules. First when picking green nuts never, even if one drops from the hand, pick any nuts up off the ground. Those that fall at this stage are almost certainly bad ones which are not worth the wear and tear on the back muscles and the time lost in bending. Secondly, I throw out from the barrow all those whose husks are suspiciously tinged with pale yellow. If not bad already they will be by the time they reach the market.

The reward: a cluster of Lamberts filbert, the Kent cob ready for the market.

Immediately after the War, for a year or two, it was permissible to send nuts to Covent Garden in 100lb sacks. That was a method with nothing to recommend it;

marketing early green nuts with any damp in the husks
could only lead to over-heating and a ruined sample. This
only lasted a year or two; thereafter there was a change to
20lb narrow hessian bags supplied by the market and that
was the system for a number of years. Later when wooden
slatted tomato trays became common their re-use to hold
10lb of nuts when well packed down became general.
These are non-returnable and the cost of trays and cover
are a charge against the price. Supplies of trays are kept
available by the various local agents for the Covent
Garden Merchants but are also usually obtainable at a
lesser charge from most well-disposed retail greengrocers
who would otherwise dispose of them as waste.[38]

Initially we sent our nuts to A.J. Edwards & Son at the
Old Covent Garden, that firm became by amalgamation
Mack and Edwards Ltd. with whom we have continued to
deal and by whom we have been well served. The
marketing charges at present are as follows:[39]

Sales commission   10% on price:
Handling charge   3p per tray:
Account service charge   50p per 100 lb:
Carriage   14p per tray:
Value added tax at 15%

To begin with bags or trays left at the front gate at
sundown were picked up by the market lorry but that was
an insecure arrangement. For a number of years now we
have delivered to a fixed collecting point, originally
Ashdown's Yard at Oldbury but subsequently at Paygate

53

in the younger Ashdown's farm on the A227 Tonbridge Road. A recent turn for the worse is that the trays have been coming through with hardboard bottoms instead of the spaced wooden slats originally used. That I consider to be a pity; the gaps between slats allowed the packed down nuts to ventilate and the earwigs, ladybirds, and other creepy crawlies which made their homes between husks and nut to creep out. We have always tried to clear our nut crop out of the way before the end of September. Possibly by doing so we have accepted a penny or so less on the price than we might have obtained in October for later harvested nuts, but I am not at all sure that overall there would be much difference in the end result, as the moisture content of the early pickings must mean fewer nuts to the pound than would be contained in the later much drier product We consider that our market wholesalers have always done very well for us, since as often as not we have been a penny or two on the right side of other growers. Indeed we should be when one looks at some of the quite appalling quality to be seen in the local shops each autumn. What we have gained, worth a great deal more than a penny or two a pound, has been the best of the September weather during which to pick. There can be few more enjoyable activities on a fine dry warm September afternoon than an hour or two spent picking nuts.[40]

And so one leaves the nuts for perhaps as much as six weeks until the leaves are down, and then the cycle begins again with the wanning to be done in the remaining days of autumn.

[40] *A record of the weight of cobnuts sent to market from 1953 to 1984 is given in Appendix 5.*

Storage

Of storage I have little to say. It may be that there are experts who can pick up ripe nuts and hold them until the market price is right; but if there are their nuts must be well harvested and the husks dried right out, otherwise unless spread in a very thin layer, they will overheat and however good the nut may be within the shell the sample will look a mess. For household use I have seen it recommended that one should plant drain pipes vertically in the garden, fill with nuts and put a tile over the top. Our own method has been to store in Kilner jars well laced with common salt having removed the husks first. I have opened one such jar after 6 years life on the shelf and have found the contents perfectly acceptable and only very mildly impregnated with the salt and that to advantage. The best and most trouble-free way of retaining a well flavoured dish for Christmas is simply to leave them outside in an open container in the weather but well within the sphere of influence of the household cats.

Earlier Patterns of Consumption

It is known that in their heyday a considerable quantity of nuts was taken by shipping companies for consumption on ocean going liners. Nuts are known to have some anti scorbutic qualities but whether that was the reason or whether they were shipped for the delectation of the passengers with time on their hands to do the cracking I have not been able to establish. There could be a link between the Heraclian nuts in the sunken amphorae and those in the dining saloons of the late 19th and early 20th

Century liners. Other outlets for the U.K. surplus were found in the export markets. In the days of Empire they were always popular with expatriates and a significant quantity went also to the United States. I have heard it said locally that in the days when they were fourpence a pound, quantities of nuts were taken up by the chemical firms who extracted a brown dye from them. Some were certainly taken up by the confectionery trade and some used for the extraction of a very special oil.[41] All these uses were dying out if not dead by 1937. Certainly if a home-grown crop reaching the market amounts to no more than two tons there is no room for commercial use.

American Culture

It is of interest to note that as the production in this country tailed off to the extent that we were no longer able to meet any demand from across the Atlantic, so they in their turn developed a local industry of their own. There, we are told, in Oregon nut plantations came into being on a very much larger scale than those to which we are accustomed here. Trees, maybe Corylus Californica, are still grown in the bush form but on a much taller leg and planted with a far wider space in between the rows and with all the land in the world over and above to spare, at a far lower number of trees to the acre. Given a width of 15ft between the rows the trees are allowed to grow upwards and the nuts shaken or allowed to fall naturally. They are then swept mechanically into rows midway

[41] *Woodland Crafts quotes the price in 1947 of a small bottle of Hazel nut oil as £1 while at the same time shelled hazel nuts were 8 shillings a pound.*

between each pair of trees. The sweeper is followed by a harvester which separates the nuts from the debris; the nuts are then dried down to an 8 -10% moisture content before then being put into store or sent to market They say in a good year The yield can be as high as 25lb per tree, giving a tonnage of 1.5 per acre. At that rate of cropping with mechanisation a team of five can harvest 200 acres in ten days. That in the New World makes commercial sense out of the one manpower pocket handkerchief form of culture of the Old.

The Story of Merrimans and its Plantation

Perusal of the abstracts of title is interesting though not of any great help in identifying the land use of the area in the mid 19th Century so as to pin point the date when the nuts were first planted. From one of these we can tell that in 1859 one Benjamin Harrison (the elder) raised the sum of £500 on mortgage from Hester Taylor, a spinster of St John's Road, Sevenoaks. This Benjamin had two sons, Benjamin and Edward.

Benjamin and his father may not have been on reasonable terms; although by his will made in 1867, Benjamin the elder appointed Benjamin the younger together with his second son, Edward and his friend William Morgan executors when he died on 23 October 1876, the younger Benjamin renounced the right to prove his father's will, and to accept any benefit thereunder.

In due course Edward and William Morgan proved the will and put the property up for sale by auction and

Edward Cazalet of Fairlawn was the purchaser.[42] On 31
December 1876 the freehold was conveyed to him by the
two proving executors in consideration of a payment of
£1,520. In the parcels clause the land and premises are
fully described by reference to the preceding occupants,
and its acreage stated to be 4 acres and 30 perch. The first
tenant or occupant to be mentioned was one Thomas
Streeton, he gave the place to Thomas Morgan and in turn
to his wife Elizabeth and finally, prior to the Harrison
executors, William Palmer was the tenant under Benjamin
the elder. There is no clue as to when Benjamin the elder[43]
acquired his freehold interest The plan on this deed shows
an area of approximately 113ft square in the north east
corner as the site of a cottage with out-buildings. The rest
of the area is shown as planted up with trees in regular
lines and not as a haphazard growth of woodland. From
knowledge of the conveyancing practice at the time I
would say that this plan indicates that the whole area was
at that time artificially planted with deciduous trees and
what other than our existing nuts could these have been?

This conclusion is borne out by the consideration stated
in the early deeds. In 1859 a prudent lender would
advance 66 2/3% of a property valuation. If Hester Taylor
adhered to that rule we get a value of £750 for the
agricultural cottage with its 4 acres. Not unreasonable if
the acres bore an established plantation producing cash
crop but out of line for a cottage in a wilderness. Again,

---

[42] *Edward at that time was described as a miner of Quartz Reef Pleasant
Creek, Australia.*
[43] *Is this Benjamin the Benjamin of Old Stones, Ightham the antiquarian?
We think not.*

in 1876, when the plantation had still further matured a price of £1520 was not unreasonable for a cottage with 4 acres of nuts.

I can therefore point with some certainty to the conclusion that our plantation was well established by 1850. What more can be deduced from the history of the varieties found in the plantation? The Cosford cob became available commercially in 1816, the Prolific from Pearsons at much the same time; Lambert's Filbert our genuine Kent cobnut was a little later and the Frizzled nut was certainly extant in some form or other, though La Bergeri obviously hybridized from it, was not brought in from Belgium until 1846. All these varieties other than La Bergeri appear with very many others in the lists of nuts grown in Chiswick in the garden of the Royal Horticultural Society in 1826 and 1831. From this I deduce that the earliest possible planting date was probably between 1830 and 1845. that would give the trees a life of nearly 150 years so far and there is plenty of vigour in most of them to ensure continued survival for a little longer. But that is not the whole of the story. When my ownership began in 1946 the southern part of my nut plantation and wood was, in common with Dole's Field lying between my southern boundary and the Ivy Hatch Church subject to a small annual payment to Queen Anne's Bounty in respect of the tithe rent charge. Such rent charges were first created by the Tithe Commutation Act of 1836 which in such a manner rationalised the payment and ultimate redemption of tithe as payment notionally of the value in cash or kind of a tenth of the produce of land under cultivation going back to time immemorial. That implies that Dole's Field and a part of what was to become the Merrimans plantation had been under cultivation well before my earliest date. Furthermore, in the hearth of the small living room in the front of what was the original cottage is a stone bearing the initials TM and the year 1807.[44] That certainly gives the impression that that was the year in which the house was built. If so, the inhabitants whoever they were had to get a living from the land. Certainly four acres of sparse lower Greensand would provide no living if any attempt was made at cereal cropping. Would such a living as early as 1807 come from a crop of cobs interplanted with soft fruits such as currants and raspberries? It is possible and if not how else did the cottagers live? Did they work the present plantation but extended as it clearly was through the area between the stream and the flank of Rosewood to Ismays Road? Or were they tenants and working for a living wage?

Fag Ends

Kent Cobs

The popularity of Lambert's Filbert over the other varieties so far as the planters in Kent were concerned lay partly in the fact that the long husk totally enclosing and

---

[44] *M is for Morgan?*

often sealing in the nut ensures the minimum loss of texture and flavour due to drying out between picking from the tree and the consumer's plate. With many other varieties abscission is not delayed and without a retaining husk the nut itself becomes detached. Thus it is easy to present a tray consisting of a variety of separated nuts mixed with their husks which originally together constituted the bunches when picked. A cluster of Lamberts will remain whole and in excellent condition long after it has been picked.

Nut dropping

The worse offender is White Lambert whose pale round nuts can be shed by the tree at the first moment of ripening. For my one tree of this variety the picking rule of ignoring those on the ground has to give way to salvage. Next on the list are the Bergeri-type trees whose frilly husks are often empty by the time one reaches them towards the end of picking. Cosford behaves fairly reasonably though for retention one must give pride of place to Lambert As between one variety and another there is a great deal of difference to be found between the zone at the top of the nut. Some are flat, others rounded and other quite markedly pointed. The rounded and pointed varieties have a well-defined point of abscission and these are the ones that are contained in their husks for the longest Lambert can even become detached from its base and yet be retained by the envelope until the stalk itself is shed.

On food value and flavour

An analysis of a sample of mixed varieties carried out in February 1983 gives the following composition: [45]

> moisture 15.5%:
> protein 14.8%:
> oil 57.25%:
> fibre 8.7%.

So clearly there is a worthwhile nutritional value. Even the fibre, which is high in the sample taken is of value as roughage. How far our indigenous cobs go into the products sold in the health food shops, nut cake, nut cutlet, nut chocolate and the like, is the producers trade secret but the probability is that such use is small and that imported nuts which are very high in nutritional value and sold at a lower price are preferrable. So also must be the case in the formation of the various muesli preparations and it could be that the Barcelona nuts meets most of these needs, adding just that crispness and crunchy texture without any evident increase in food value or flavour. In the eyes of some a diet based mainly on nuts is one of the marks of a food faddist. At one of the darker periods of the 1939-45 War the late Lord Woolton, the nation's housekeeper, was forced to recommend in Cabinet a tightening of the rationing system and the advocation of a degree of self-

---

[45] *By courtesy of Alan Graham of W.& C. Scott Ltd. Co. Tyrone, Northern Ireland.*

help by the resort to the edible products of nature to supplement the national larder. Winston Churchill to whom all forms of faddism were anathema put that suggestion down with one of his wilder generalisations by stating with emphasis that all the food faddists he had ever known, nut eaters and the like had died young after a long period of senile decay. Perhaps after 40 years we have managed to prolong the longevity and slow down the senility as the supply of home-grown nuts had faded away. As to flavour, most of us are familiar with the expression "a nutty taste" but what I ask myself is a nutty taste? True, nuts of whatever type have a taste and there is all the difference in the world between the taste of a monkey nut, a Brazil nut, a walnut, a chestnut and a cob nut. The first four have distinctive tastes if that be the same as flavour of their own; the Kent cob in all varieties has a taste and flavour too, albeit a very faint one to my palate and none of them seem to have a flavour in common with the others. They do however have what most of us for lack of a better word would describe as an attractive crunchiness. That seems to be more a matter of texture so perhaps what we mean by a nutty taste is merely a nutty texture plus a faint individual flavour. To me, Kent cobs have very little to offer; others would disagree and are perhaps more fortunate in the sensitivity of their palate. I would say that the smaller the nut the better the quality and some would say the sweeter; that would put the wild hazel at the top of the list with Purpurae a good second and the White Lambert not far behind. Certainly there is all the difference in the world between a Kent cob cracked and eaten straight off the tree at the moment of ripening and the same nut left in a dish in the dry of the house until Christmas and then cracked and eaten in a shrivelled state. Not that I decry my nuts at Christmas, though I do maintain that it is the charm of the festive season that adds a lot to their acceptability. The best cob of all in my opinion is one that has been popped into a crevice by some bird or beastie and allowed to ripen to the point of germination. I come across them in my dry-stone walls from time to time and very good they are when on the point of bursting out of their shell. Each to his own taste is very true of our English nuts; it is for every individual to make up his or her mind about them and if you find you differ in every word of the foregoing no one will be less surprised than the writer.

What of the Future?

Commercially in this country one can only say with sorrow that there is none for the home-grown crop, though the importation of Barcelona nuts for the confectionery and Christmas trade seems likely to continue. [46] Whatever home grown nuts are produced today can easily be absorbed by the domestic market. In the longer term what survival there is to be may well be confined to the larger gardens in the country where the labour situation permits

[46] *Syn. Red Lambert.*

small nurseries to be maintained as interesting features and perhaps in one or two nurseries for stock. For the nurserymen or garden centre enterprises to hold stocks of different varieties in any quantity is more likely to be the exception rather than the general rule. If obtainable, in any garden where fruit is grown in variety, a group of nuts say of half a dozen trees in a circular plan, containing perhaps Lamberts Filbert, a Cosford, a La Bergeri, a While Lambert, one of the best of the Webbs and with a Purpura in the centre would be an interesting feature which if allowed to go to full height would also earn its keep by providing much of the staking and hedge repairing material required elsewhere. Indeed in the wild or allowed to revert to the wild as in many places is happening today the future may be only as a coppice material for rotational cutting. The old art of the woodland craftsman calling for the use of the supple well grown two-year wands and the split rods to form inter-woven hurdles will still have their place in the rural economy. The sheep are still with us and there is no reason to think that the age of the plastic hurdle is upon us yet.

As long as quality can be maintained the English nut be it cob or filbert presented in prime condition and in such quantity as are available will always command a good price. To those who know there is no comparison between that and the bags of the dried up shrivelled imported product one sees in every greengrocers shop from November onwards. For ordinary garden culture it would be wrong not to stress that the purple nut is, when its colour is at its best in May and June, as ornamental as any tree or shrub of special hue for blending with the greenery of any part of the garden devoted to shrubs.[47] This variety has in my experience the ability to grow fairly quickly to maturity. It is a true Filbert, the nuts are small, are well flavoured and the shell is curiously pointed at both ends. The "major" in the name appears to refer to the size of the leaf which against that of other varieties is huge, rather than the nut. Perhaps for any garden with a leaning towards the grotesque mention should be made of the variety which used to be known as Sir Harry Lauder's walking stick or corkscrew nut to be an interesting oddity at best

[47] *Corylus major purpurea.*

"Tot homines, quot sententies"

Appendix 1

Possible location of nut plantations in the Ightham area

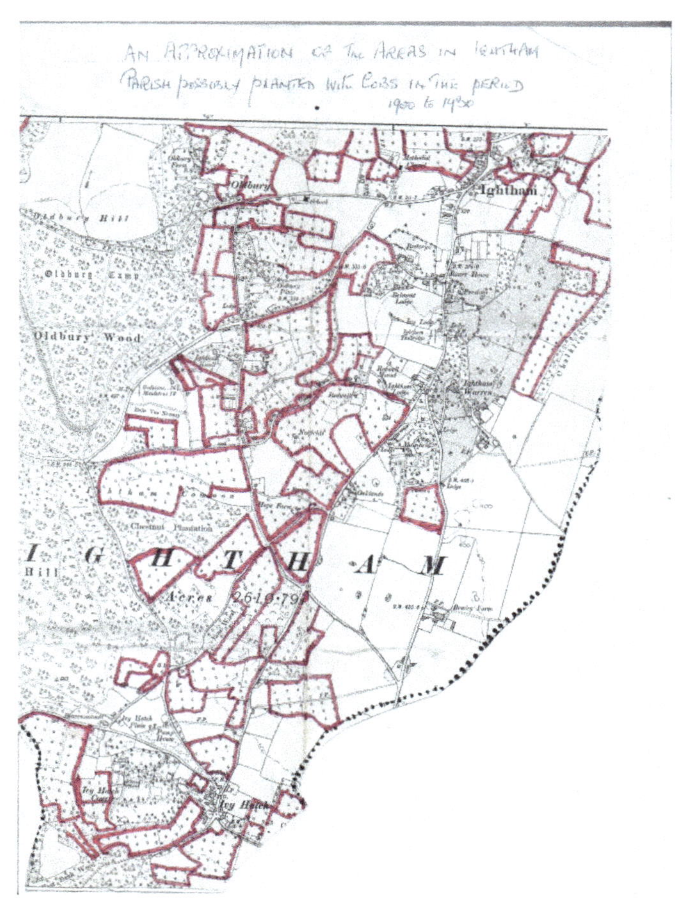

Appendix 2

THE KENT INCORPORATED SOCIETY FOR PROMOTING EXPERIMENTS IN HORTICULTURE
(A COMPANY LIMITED BY GUARANTEE)

EAST MALLING RESEARCH STATION
EAST MALLING
MAIDSTONE
KENT
ME19 6BJ

DIRECTOR
I J GRAHAM-BRYCE D PHIL
SECRETARY R L OXLEY MBIM

YOUR REF

OUR REF 20.2 LD

TELEPHONE
WEST MALLING 843833
(STD CODE 0732)
TELEGRAMS
RESEARCH EAST MALLING

LIAISON DEPARTMENT

15th September, 1982

Dear Mr. Green,

Coryulus nuts

Thank you for your letter of 8th September. I have to admit that we did not know of your collection or we would have passed all of our enquiries on to you!

We do have an appreciable amount of literature or the subject of cobs which you are very welcome to study. It varies from chapters in older books on the cultivation through various bibliographies to MAFF bulletins and Jaynes 'Handbook of North American Nut Trees'.

Unfortunately, we have no experts on hazel nuts here, those who had a wide knowledge have retired. Mr. Garner, our propagating officer for many years is still active and lives in East Malling village, it would probably be advantageous to consult him. Otherwise I think that you might get some help from the RHS gardens at Wisley. Mr. Baker would be the man to contact. Apart from these two I suspect that you are the expert.

As I said previously, we would be quite happy for you to visit our library; would you please let our Librarian, Peter Blundred, know when to expect you.

Yours sincerely,

M.E. Cook

W. Green Esq.,
Merrimans,
Sandy Lane Ivy Hatch,
SEVENOAKS,
Kent

AJM:

Appendix 3: Development of pollination in Lamberts Filbert

8 January 1983. Catkins tightly shut, leaf buds but no nutkins.

23 January 1983. Catkins beginning to open at base, some yellow pollen.

6 February 1983. After an exceptionally warm January; catkins fully open, pollen flying, nutkins have appeared.

27 February 1983. After two weeks snow and frost; catkins now mostly brown with no pollen, nutkins with prominent red tips, leaf buds swelling.

27 February 1983. In contrast the later flowering La Bergeri type has fully open catkins with pollen flying, prominent nutkins and leaf buds.

Appendix 4: The Allen Scythe

The Allen Scythe was manufactured by John Allen and Sons of Oxford between 1935 and 1972. This picture shows the standard wheelbase with the side cut attachment.

Appendix 5: Production record

From our beginning in 1947 until 1952 no records were kept but these years included the one of the caterpillars, one when we went away in early September and unauthorised helpers picked the crop and one which was almost a total wipe-out owing to a snowy winter when the snow stayed with us until 25th March. I do not mean that the other years were very famous though they included the one when the mice cleared the tea chests. Thereafter I have kept records, if only to establish a loss if the taxman commented. These are as follows:

Quantity sent to market

	lbs		lbs		lbs		lbs
		1960	1200	**1970**	1000	**1980**	520
		1961	100	**1971**	270	**1981**	360
		1962	60	**1972**	520	**1982**	870
1953	660	**1963**	200	**1973**	350	**1984**	830
1954	400	**1964**	20	**1974**	600		
1955	320	**1965**	520	**1975**	180		
1956	1500	**1966**	620	**1976**	990		
1957	200	**1967**	920	**1977**	1200		
1958	1200	**1968**	800	**1978**	260		
1959	600	**1969**	20	**1979**	220		

9 780095 437689 5